TOWNSENDS

A SHOWMAN'S STORY

By Kay Townsend

First published in 2006

Reprinted 2007

© Kay Townsend
Email: kay58@fsmail.net

ISBN 10: 0-9553593-0-3

ISBN 13: 978-0-9553595-0-7

Cover design and print by

Creeds the Printers, Broadoak, Bridport, Dorset DT6 5NL

CONTENTS

RICHARD TOWNSEND & SONS
FUN FAIR

WILL VISIT

ILMINSTER CARNIVAL

OCT 5. 6. 7.

SUPER DODG'EMS · SWINGS

and a GREAT VARIETY OF FIRST CLASS

AMUSEMENTS

EVENINGS at 6.30   **SATURDAYS at 2.30**

INTRODUCTION

I come from a family of West Country showmen. When I was young, I loved listening to the old stories. I found them so interesting that when I was 11 years old I made notes, of all the things I did not want to forget.

Now 36 years later, I was talking to a gentleman recently, I told him a story from years ago. He said, "Kay you must write this down, people want to know this."

At the end of the summer season in 2004, I found myself starting to type and supposedly only doing this book for the family, especially the children. However, people have been asking, "When is it going to be finished? We would like a copy". So now, I am doing this book for everyone.

Every now and then, you will come across 'Did You Knows?', which will contain interesting facts as you follow the story. I hope you find our story interesting and a pleasure to read. Therefore, with the help of my family, this is our showman's story to you.

CHAPTER 1

1829 – Our Beginning

On February 18th 1829,
at St Mary's Church,
Oxford,
the marriage of
Henry Townsend & Lydia Dixon.

To them was born a son
in September 1834 at Witney,
Oxfordshire.
They called him
William Townsend.

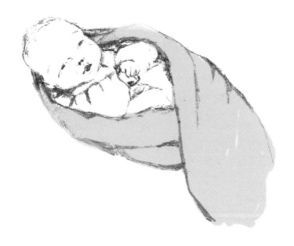

What We Know Of William's Life

William spent his childhood living in the High Street at Witney, Oxfordshire.

On 26th July 1856, he married a Miss Ann Ford, who was the daughter of a tucker at a local blanket factory, and was living in Corn Street. William and Ann were both 22 yrs old.

One year later in 1857 their first child was born, Joseph William. For the first few years of their married life, the couple remained on Corn Street. Ann worked in the Witney blanket factory at Witney and William became a hawker just like his father.

Corn Street (By kind permission of Oxfordshire Studies Library).

Then four years later, according to the 1861 Somerset Census, William and Ann had moved, and were living in an old caravan at Christchurch Frome, Somerset. Now William was a <u>travelling</u> hawker.

Ten years later in 1871, the National Census declared that William and Ann both 37 years old, had moved again and were now a family with seven children. They all were living in an old <u>caravan</u> next door to the ironmongers near the Bell Inn pub, in the market place at Radstock near Bath.

William's occupation was now Coachman/Carrier on the mail stagecoach between Radstock and Bath, leaving daily at 8:30 am and returning at 4:30 pm. It is believed that Ann became a china and glass dealer.

Circa 1800-1900 mail stage. Sketch by Carolyn Herbert.

By 1875, railways became more widespread, and then mail was transported by train, so William soon lost his job. So now William had very little, and the big worry was money and how to survive. The profits from selling a little glass and china would not have been enough to keep his family-of now 9 children.

William came up with the idea of a small children's Round-a-bout. We are unsure whether he bought a small children's Round-a-bout (juvenile ride to us) or if he made one himself. However, what we do know is the little Round-a-bout was to shape the next five generations of the Townsend family.

So William, with his little ride, actually started our journey of what was to become...

A SHOWMAN'S STORY

By now, William and Ann would have had two small caravans/wagons each being about 14ft long. The old wagons were made up of a single skin of thin board. Their children told later, of how in the winter, they sometimes woke up to find frost on their blankets. Their cooking would have been done outside on a fire, as the wagons were mainly for sleeping in.

William's little ride was simple, nothing fancy and very basic; it packed on a cart, and was pulled by a horse. This horse also pulled the Round-a-bout around, in order for the children to have their ride.

And as for William's children, when travelling to the next fair, they had to walk behind the cart. Some of these fairs would have been local charter fairs where horses and cattle were sold on the street.

William and Ann had nine children, one of whom was Richard, my grandfather, and it is Richards's lifeline that this story will eventually follow.

Did You Know?

The early rides that were seen at the fairs were swinging boats, very <u>small</u> children's Round-a-bouts, and a small wheel, all of which had very little detail and would look very basic, even untidy, and not painted like fairground rides are today.

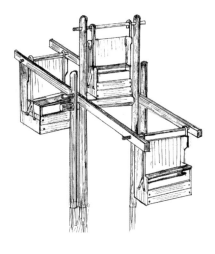

Sketch by Ann Townsend.
Wheel circa 1700s.

Sketch by Carolyn Herbert.

Round-a-bout circa 1805
(legless horses would have
been all around the edge).

Later, the cog was more widely used, so the ride would then be turned by a handle.   Remember the Round-a-bouts were not as big as they are today, and it was not until 1863 that Frederick Savage of Kings Lynn introduced steam power to drive them.

*An early pony-driven Round-a-bout, from Oxfordshire
(By kind permission of the Fairground Heritage Trust).*

Charter Fairs

William would have attended Charter Fairs with his little ride, which were a particular fairs/markets that had existed for hundreds of years, having been awarded a royal charter by the King. The dates these fairs were held on each year, had to be as stipulated in the charter, and could not be changed.

These markets/fairs would attract all sorts-freak shows, Jesters and fortune-tellers and they also attracted the undesirable beggars and pickpockets.

If for any reason one year is missed, or the fair does not take place on the date as stipulated in the charter, then the charter is broken. Then the local Council can stop the fair ever taking place again. If a fair has become a nuisance in the eyes of the local Council, they have been known to take advantage of this by not allowing a fair to return in the future.

When I was a child, we attended a Charter Fair in the square at Beaminster, Dorset. However after many years, the family decided not to hold the fair. We knew that once the decision was made, that was it, as the Council would not allow us to return.

Family History So Far

Henry Townsend
Occupation: Hawker
Married In 1829
Lydia Dixon

Their Son...

William Townsend
Born 1834
Married In 1856
Ann Ford
Became Travelling Hawker,
Mail Stage Driver,
Then Travelling Showman

Their Son...

(Next) Chapter Two
Richard Townsend
Born 1866, Showman.
(my grandfather)

CHAPTER 2

1866

From now on this story concentrates on William & Ann's seventh child Richard, who was my granddad.

My grandfather, Richard Townsend was born in 1866 at Weston-Super-Mare. He was the 7th of 9 children born to William and Ann Townsend.

We know very little of Richard's childhood.

In the 1881 Census, William and Ann declared that all of their children were scholars, but I have my doubts about this being true, due to the travelling. Also Richard was unable to read or write, and he could only just sign his name.

We know that as a young man, Richard left home and joined a menagerie, which I believe was a mixture of a circus and a fair, with street shows/entertainers and jugglers and performing animals.

However, he was not gone for long. And when he returned home, Richard built himself a stall and later a set of swinging boats. Along with his father (William) he would open around Dorset and Somerset fairs, travelling with every thing he had packed on a cart.

Ten years later, in the 1891 Census William and Ann were still travelling and were at West Street, Bridport, Dorset, both now 46 years old, with their little ride. Their son Richard now being 25 years, had his swing boats, a shooter stall and a paper organ.

When Richard Met Kate

In 1895, Richard, at the age of 29 and still at home with parents (William and Ann), he opened with his swing boats behind the Quicksilver Mail pub in Yeovil, Somerset.   The fair ground organ at the time was playing 'two little girls in blue'; and Richard happened to notice a young lady dressed in blue. Her name was Kate Forse, daughter of James Cox Forse, a local landlord. Richard was able to talk to Kate for a while, and eventually he met Kate's father.

James Forse got along well with Richard, and always made him feel welcome, and soon Richard and Kate were courting.

Kate was 19 and she was a Sunday School teacher. She had a good education for a landlord's daughter.

In 1896 not long after the couple met, Kate's father, James Forse died and so Kate's life began with Richard. (Over the next 50 years, Kate's education and brilliant mind for business, helped shape R. Townsend & Sons' future which you will notice throughout this story.)

At the start of their life together they had very little, only Richard's swinging boats and stall, and for a while they still travelled around attending various fairs with his parents William and Ann. In about 1896, Richard was one of the first people to pull a horse and wagon on the Bridport fairground. Before this, he told a reporter from the Dorset Echo, he could also remember opening in Bridport when horses and cattle were sold on the pavements in West Street, and Round-a-bouts opened outside the Greyhound Hotel.

On returning from the fair on the Island of Portland in 1899, their first child was born. Kate went into labour when they reached Wyke Regis. So James Richard Townsend was born 9th November 1899 in a small wagon at Foords Corner, Wyke Regis, Weymouth.

First born, James Richard (was always known as Dick).

In the 1901 Census, Richard and Kate were still travelling with his father William, as the Census declared in at Damers Road, Dorchester, two vans one occupied by William and Ann, and their 3 daughters and the other by Richard and Kate, and baby James, aged 2.

Unfortunately Kate was not happy. She was educated and this caused conflict with Richard's family, so after a family disagreement Richard and Kate decided to go it alone. When open at Bridport Fair, William said to Richard "We are going back to Lyme Regis after this fair"

Richard said "You can, but me and Kate are going to Weymouth" so in about 1905, with what little they had pulled by a horse, they made their way to Weymouth.

(THEY WOULD NOT HAVE KNOWN THEN, THAT IT WAS THE BEST THING THEY EVER DID!)

After a while, they managed to rent a piece of land along Weymouth harbour side (now a car park) in Commercial Road.

Over the next 50 years with Kate's mind for business and Richard's hard work, they built up the business known as R. Townsend & Sons. They became known and respected by many people; they built a life that shaped the generations to come.

After baby James Richard (Dick) was born in November 1899, in their wagon at Wyke Regis, later to follow was:

Thomas William born 1902,
Swanage Cottage Hospital, cost 10 shillings.

Hilda Kathleen, born 1905 and Albert John (Pat),
born 1906 at Commercial Road, Weymouth.

Doris Linda born 1911 at Newstead Road, Weymouth.

(Triplets)

Joseph (Joe) Harold (above), Kate Ruby & Mona Pearl.

Born January 1914 in their showman's wagon alongside the harbour in Commercial Road, Weymouth.

Kate received the Kings Sovereign as triplets were rarely born, however the two girl triplets did not survive.

Joe seen here in centre being held by Nurse Honeybun (Joe later became my dad).

On August 16th 1912, at the age of 78, Richard's father, William Townsend died. At the time, his wagon was in a field next to the silk factory at Sherborne, as he had just attended the fair. As soon as Richard received the news of his father's death he rode his horse 30 miles from Weymouth to Sherborne and had to arrange for his father to buried in the Sherborne Cemetery. Remember, it was William in Chapter One who started our story with his little ride.

Ann ended her days in a place called Burden's Buildings here in Weymouth. This was regarded as poorhouse. She died 3 years after William and she is buried in Weymouth.

CHAPTER 3

1905 – Building A Business

In about 1905, when Richard and Kate left William at Bridport, they eventually ended up in Commercial Road Weymouth. This is where the business started to grow, as Richard and Kate managed to buy their <u>first</u> ride. Richard realised that from the nearby Island of Portland, which was a naval docks, many sailors would come into port, and needed more entertainment than just the little fair that they had, and there was more money to be made if they had a ride. So in 1908, he bought a small three-abreast set of Gallopers, from William Wilson. One of the problems he had was that the sailors would always go to the pub with their girl friends and get a little tipsy before coming to the fair. Then, when riding, they would climb up the brass rods as they were going around on the gallopers and so try to get up in the rafters of the ride. So Richard put chicken wire above/in the top.

In 1908 when Richard and Kate bought their first set of gallopers, the ride was at its most popular peak, It was the central attraction, as crowds of people in their 'Sunday best' would climb aboard the horses and listen to the organ music, while children would buy confetti for 1 penny a pocket full, which was thrown when the ride was in motion, to create an atmosphere they could only experience at the fair.

Their First Gallopers

(Richard)

In 1909, they were able to buy their first traction engine, *'Empress of the South'* 2562. An 8 n.h.p Burrell, weighing about 14 tons.

So now the family would venture out from Commercial Road, to local fairs and fetes, but always returning. We know that only days before the outbreak of the First World War, they were open at a fete at Upwey, near Weymouth, as a local caption under a picture of people happily riding on their Gallopers at the event said "Little did these people know that in two days time we would be at war". Leaving Commercial Road occasionally came to an end, as the *'Empress'* was requisitioned in 1914 by the War Department.

'*Empress of the South*', after the War Department requisitioned her. Seen here helping at Wilton in Wiltshire in 1914.

W. Nichols had her during the requisition days, with his name on her canopy. After the war, she was back travelling again, as it has been recorded in 1920, she was travelling with Chair-o-planes, which my family did have for a short time.

Commercial Road served them well, as they were able to raise their children, all 6 of them. As the local school in School Street was not far, Kate wanted her children to have some sort of education like herself.

The cost was 2d a week, so all their children were taught how to read and write, not with pen and paper, but with a board and chalk. Although I can remember my dad Joe would read the newspaper, and would sign his name, but would never write a letter to anyone.

1914 was a year that Kate and Richard would never forget, as in the January Kate gave birth to the last of their children (a set of triplets - Joseph, Kate and Mona) in their wagon in Commercial Road. Then, only a few days later, the two baby girls died, leaving only baby Joseph who was small, but strong, (Joseph became my dad).

Then in August, when the First World War broke out and the Government requisitioned the '*Empress of the South*', and times became hard again, money was short, as they were not taking good money any more in Commercial Road.

Their first-born son Dick was now 16, so he went to Wilton with the '*Empress of the South*'. Dick was not very good at getting up early and so he had many a telling-off. He eventually joined the Army to fight and like many lads, he did not tell the truth about his age.

He was wounded in the leg by a sniper not long after joining, and for three days he was trapped on barbed wire before being found.

Kate also decided whilst in Commercial Road that it would be better if they named the business RICHARD TOWNSEND & SONS, as they had 6 children now, James(Dick), Thomas, Albert (Pat), Hilda, Doris and Joe.

Determined to survive the hardships of the war, they came up with another idea in 1918, by applying to the Council to put a small Round-a-bout on Weymouth sands; this was just before the war was over. This Round-a-bout became a part of Weymouth's history (more about this in chapter four).

1918

Now the war was over. The family, being young, managed to pull through the hardship of war, and there was some celebration, as they were back in business again. Unfortunately, money was still short, as the punters never had much money to spend. The world economy was so poor after the First War, and things were not the same. By the end of 1918 Dick, now recovered from his war injury, was 19, and it was discovered that he was going to be the fine painter of the family. So much of his time now would be spent painting the Galloper.

Richard in about 1918 sold his first set of Gallopers to Joe Brewer (of South Wales) and the next ride he bought was from a Mr Ted Fear, of Bristol, this was a Switchback ride.

However, Richard then discovered after paying cash for it, that Mr Fear still owed money to the previous owner. Therefore, the ride turned out to be expensive, as Richard paid off the remaining debt.

Like all showmen, their children had to help within the business. It was a hard life; therefore I can not imagine them having much of a childhood; however, they did have some good times, as I have heard my Uncle Tom say, that as children, they got up to all sorts. The two girls of the Family, Doris and Hilda, were both very beautiful. At fetes, they would enter competitions, like the most beautiful ankles, and Doris would usually win.

Doris   *Hilda*

Then one day at a fete, they came across 'Count the notches on the stick' to win. Doris would distract the man by talking to him, while the others would count the notches!

'Empress of the South',
Towing, however, it still had W Nichols on her canopy.

We are unsure of the date, but it was about 1921 when the family sold the *'Empress Of The South'*. They then owned another three engines in the next 10 Years, which were *St Bernard HT2959*, a small Garrett 4 CD compound 5 and a half ton 4 n h p tractor. Works number 31110 (not to be confused with the Herbert St Bernard).

Jellicoe II PR8184 A Burrell 7 and a half-ton compound 3-speed tractor.

Princess FX7170 A Fowler works number 12255; she was a 5 n h p weighing 10 ton. We converted her to a showman's, and finally retired her in 1946.

(More about the Princess in Chapter Five 'The Steam and Our Queen.')

Richard had the switchback ride 3 years now. Having to pay off the debt of Mr Fear, It cost him dearly. We presume the family did not like the ride, as after only 3 years, he sold the ride on.

An advertisement from a 1921 'World's Fair' *'For sale: 30ft switchback, made by Savages, Kings Lynn. 8 cars, seats 48 grown up persons. All complete, without organ or trucks. Reason for selling, bought Gallopers. Apply R Townsend, Commercial Rd, Weymouth'.*

So 1921, Richard acquired his last set of Gallopers from, it is thought, Studts of Wales. This set was more ornate as you can see.

This was a 'Tidmans' set, which was cut down from a 4-abreast to a 3. Also, Richard acquired a new 89-key Verbeeck organ in 1924, which must have been for this set.

Also in the early 1920's, Richard managed to purchase his next big ride, a set of Chair-o-planes. These were steam driven. They also had an organ in the centre. Therefore, with the gallopers, they now had two big riding machines.

In the mid 1920s, it was decided to leave Commercial Road for good and start travelling again. More money was needed, and they would have to travel to find it. As Commercial Road had been their home all year round, they also now needed somewhere to stop during the winter.

When the summer season was over, a local farmer, Mr Symmons of Buckland Ripers, would allow them to pull every thing they had on his farm. (Tom later said they were the happiest days of his life in Buckland Ripers.) Also while wintering there, they discovered another form of income for the winter months, by cutting trees from Tatton copse, and selling them on as logs throughout the winter. Deliveries were made by horse and cart. Despite this there were still times when they had little money, but the farmer was good to them, and allowed them to help themselves to whatever vegetables they wanted from his field.

Although the selling of the logs in the winter made only a small amount of money, you will see later in (Chapter Nine) that timber would become an important part of life for them.

Everything was going well. They were far from well off, but the money was slowly coming in again...

Richard's travelling covered four counties Devon, Dorset, Somerset and Wiltshire; they would stay in a village or town for the fetes and shows for one or sometimes two weeks.

They had also now acquired a coconut shy, and after all this time still had their swinging boats, and a shooter stall. So apart from having to keep the traction engine stoked up to provide the power for the lights, everyone else was taking money on something when open, and they also had men working for them, as money takers on the Gallopers.

One of the ways they would attract the punters to the fair was to buy a pig for 10 shillings and have a competition. whoever sang the best song, and could hold the pig under their arm throughout the <u>whole</u> of the song, would win the pig. There had to be three contestants in order to hold the competition. The Galloper steps were used as a stage, and it has been known that if Richard found out who was going to sing, he would take them to the pub first and get them a little tipsy, so when they were singing and the pig would wriggle and squeal, they would drop the pig, and so not win the competition. A pig would last a few weeks by doing this.

However, eventually someone would win, and with the excitement of winning, they would usually drop the pig, and the pig would always run away. It was comical, watching the winner run all around the field trying to catch his pig.

I suppose that was part of the fun, and why the punters always came. When open at Weston Zoyland near Bridgwater, they decided to put on horse racing to draw the crowds, however only one horse turned up, so they gave up on that idea.

They also had other showmen join them with shows. One family with their show, would stand in front, and call 'COME AND SEE THE THREE-LEGGED LADY WITH THREE LEGS UP TO HER THIGHS; Apparently, soldiers in the 1920s were only too eager to pay, and see a girl with three legs; they entered the show with a big grin on their faces. However, their faces were a picture when they came out, as inside was a female DUCK that had three legs. Then there was the fortune-teller, the punters thought it was unbelievable what she was saying (she was drunk).

Another show that travelled with them was, 'JIM BENNET THE MAN WITH 2...' This got the punters curious-2 of what? On paying their money and entering, they found it was a man with 2 thumbs.

So yes, sometimes other families would travel with Townsend's for a while, the Whitelegg family and Banjo Edwards, Tommy Clements, George and Flo Symmons, Charlie Connelly and Billy Hallet were just a few. They would all pay Richard a small rent/pitch fee, as he would have to pay a farmer or the Council for the use of the field for the duration of the fair. However if Richard could see the families had not done well, he would waive the rent, as he and Kate knew what it was like not to take money in this business.

Richard did not have the Chair-o-planes for long, as in the late 20s while open in a field here in the village of Chickerell, a freak whirlwind storm blew the complete top off the Chair-o-planes.

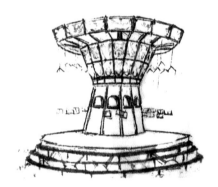

The top was never found. Very close by is a stretch of water called the Fleet which flows out to sea, so we have always presumed the top ended up in the English Channel as it was never found. So now, they were down to only one big ride again, their faithful Gallopers.

'Princess' seen here only running the lights
(Courtesy of the Fair Ground Heritage Trust).

North Curry 1939. The horse was named Prince.
Water tank and empty coal sacks, so this horse and cart kept the engines going
(Courtesy of Mr C Quick).

What Happened To Our Gallopers?

The family know that <u>one</u> set of our Gallopers, (we do not know which set) possibly after our ownership, ended up with the Elstree Film Studios. However, when the filming had finished, the Gallopers were taken to a field and the film company burnt the whole ride. We do not know the name of the film.

CHAPTER 4

1918 – Weymouth Sands

This was the start of the other side of Richard Townsend & Sons.

In 1918, nine months before the end of the First War, Richard and Kate came up with another idea. Richard approached Weymouth Council to ask if he could take a small children's Round-a-bout on Weymouth sands.

It was just a small hand turned ride on its own, which consisted of small horses.

The first ride circa 1918.

In the Committee minutes from April 1918 it states:

Resolved

That permission be granted that Mr R Townsend to place a Round-a-bout on the sands as from Monday May 13th at a weekly rent of £1.

When Richard and Kate first had a children's Round-a-bout on Weymouth beach, it was situated near the Jubilee clock end of the beach, then later moved to the pavilion end.

During the early years as there was no shed in order to pack the ride away at night, every evening Kate would take the little horses off the ride, wrap them in blankets and bury them in the sand. Then each morning she would dig them up, and put them back on the ride. Because the little Round-a-bout was doing well on the beach, Richard decided he also wanted swinging boats to stand beside the Round-a-bout, and this was the outcome:

Resolved

February 17th 1920.

That Mr R Townsend be granted sites on the sands for juvenile Round- a- bout, and juvenile swings, as from and including Easter week, to the end of the season all at a rent of £160.

You will notice the high increase in rent in such a short time (2 years).

In February 1923, the rent increased to £200.

At first, he had six swinging boats, later increased to eight…

In the last chapter, I mentioned that in the mid 1920s, Richard had left Commercial Road and started to travel again with the gallopers, in order to take more money.

However, Kate did not travel, she stayed in Weymouth to look after the beach rides during the summer, which was May until September, while Richard would travel with the fair. To be close to the beach, Kate first rented a house in New Street, and then later she bought a house nearby, 1 Market Street.

Some time later, the first ride was replaced with this one.

This ride was more sturdy, and larger, but was still <u>hand-turned at first</u>. It had little horses and cockerels with the brass rods down through their centres, they gently swung out as the ride turned.

The actual truck/centre of this ride was on large cart/spoke wheels. Because these wheels were delicate, the centre was transported to the beach each year on a flat 4-wheel truck. Then, wherever they decided the ride was going to be built, the sand would be scraped away until they found wet sand underneath. Then two old railway sleepers would be laid down on the wet sand, and the centre truck wheels would be pushed on to the sleepers.

This was for levelling purposes and to stop the wheels from sinking in the sand *(picture courtesy of Mr Gary Smart).*

I am not sure when this picture taken, but you will note the electric pole on the beach, so by this time the ride was no longer hand turned. Electricity was brought down from the Esplanade.

Now, 240volt would enter a large converter, which was nearby and 110volts would be transferred from the large converter across to the Round-a-bout, by a wire buried in a very deep trench in the sand, leading to the ride, with a motor in the centre of the ride to drive it.

The same ride above, but at a later date, the horses were removed from this ride and platforms were added, so the same little ride now had cars and animals bolted down onto the platforms. You will also notice there are new rounding boards.

Taken in 1978, my daughter Joe, aged 3.

Notice the little horses on the platforms in the picture above? These were off this ride originally, now with the brass rods removed, and we attached blocks underneath on their bellies so we were able to continue using them on the ride, by bolting them down to the platforms.

Six of these horses stayed on the ride in Weymouth and six went travelling with the fair on my Father's ride. The horses are in retirement now, but we still have those horses in the family today.

The family had a small Round-a-bout on Weymouth beach for many years, and only stopped doing so for a time, which was during the Second World War.

Over the years, there have been 3 Mrs Townsend's on the beach:-

From 1918 until 1939 there was <u>Kate</u>. Then after the Second World War, in 1948, with Kate older now, Frank and <u>Lydia</u> Townsend took over for the next 20 years. Then in 1968 Pat and <u>Phyllis</u> Townsend took over.

In the 1920s, a lady called Nancy Symonds would come to Weymouth with her grandchildren to sell her fish. She would leave her grandchildren with Kate to look after on the beach. The children were well behaved and would sit by the prom wall, waiting for their grandmother, and when the Round-a-bout was not busy, Kate would call them over to have a ride. This picture was taken when they were having one of those rides.

Memories, 1925.

This picture was given to me by one of the children in the boat, (Mary) as a black glass photo plate; I knew there was something lovely behind it – as you can see I was right. The paintwork was by James (Uncle Dick).

I know many people have childhood memories of rides on the beach, so Kate and Richard's idea back in 1918 has become a part of Weymouth's history.

Did You Know?

Normally swinging boats have a stake at each leg, as when the swings are swinging up high the legs need to be kept firmly down. However, you cannot use stakes in sand, as they would just slide out and not keep the leg down.

So this is what they do: dig a hole in front each leg, then fill a empty 10 gallon can with sand, attach one end of a chain to the can, and the other end to the leg, then drop the can in the hole and bury it. The weight of the buried can keeps the leg down.

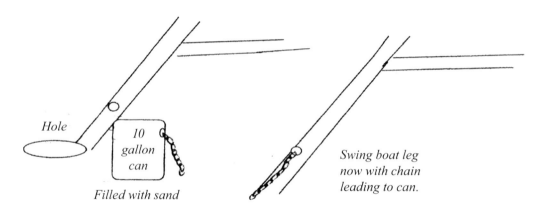

Hole

10 gallon can

Filled with sand

Swing boat leg now with chain leading to can.

Stakes

I remember Uncle Tom telling me that once when building the swinging boats up on the Fair Ground, he hit a water main while staking the boats down, water shot up out of the ground like a fountain.

Years ago when we attended a Charter Fair at the Square, Beaminster, Dorset. We had little tiny stakes especially made to keep the stalls down, in fact that's what we called them, 'the Beaminster stakes', as it was the only place we used them. The stakes had to be really short, as under the car park there would have been electricity and water mains. We were not popular with the Council, as on Monday morning after the fair, they would have to come and fill in all the little holes we had made all over the car park.

CHAPTER 5

1921-1948 – The Steam & Our Queen

They had come along way since owning their first engine *'Empress of the South'* in 1909, then selling her in 1921. In fact, they had owned 3 others since then. A Burrell, *Jellico II PR8184*, and Garrett, St Bernard HT2959, and Fowler *Princess FX7170*.

Princess

Built 1910, we purchased her in about 1921, and converted her to a showman's. She was mainly used for towing on the road, but also could run the stall lights with her dynamo when needed.

Also, it was her winch they would use to winch out any trucks that were stuck in the fields. Muddy fields are the one thing showmen could never avoid.

Fowler *'Princess'*. 12255, FX7170, she was D2 class compound 5 n h p weighing 10 tons. Seen here with broken axle, en route from Axminster to Dorchester. Pat Townsend is on the far left.

The Princess always towed the living wagon on behind. For some years, James (Dick) the eldest, and Joe, the youngest of Richard's sons, would drive the *'Princess'* on the road together. However, the two brothers did not get on well at all, so why on earth the family made them work together on the road we don't know. They would argue about something, and then would stop the *'Princess'* get off and have a punch up in the road, and then they would sit on the grass verge and refuse to get back on the engine with one another.

Meanwhile, in front, the *'Queen Mary'* had pulled in the new field. With travel being so slow, every one was gasping for a cup of tea, but the wagon was with James, Joe, and the *'Princess'*, which was now stood still on a road somewhere. Richard kept a pony and trap for a while, so Richard would ride back to find them and get them back together on the engine again. James and Joe were well known for their punch-ups on the road, yet the family continued to put them together. We have often wondered why?

James (Dick) was the eldest and Joe the youngest.

The *'Princess'* 1934

The *'Princess'*, still exists today, however she is not a showman's any more, and has been converted again by her present owners.

In 1927 the road locomotive tax doubled, from £30 to £60, which must have been a big shock to the family, when you consider they only charged 6d (six pence) a ride, so that was a lot of riders needed just to pay for the road tax.

'Queen Mary'

The Wall Street Crash in 1929 affected much of Europe. This country was really suffering by 1931.

Therefore, the Depression was the next setback the family had to conquer.

There was little money to be spent at the fairs, but Richard still managed to keep everything on the road.

Then in about 1931, they made an offer on two traction engines that came up for sale at a Portland quarry.

These were the last two engines the family bought, One was originally called 'Nellie', then later known as the 'Queen Mary'. we are unsure of the name of the other engine. The asking price was £15 each, but Uncle Tom offered them £25 for the pair, and two days later the quarry sent a messenger to say the offer was accepted. Uncle Tom said, "So we only went to buy one, but ended up with both".

The engines had been hauling stone for F J Barnes, not far from us on the Island of Portland. The unnamed engine of the pair, we sold to another showman. The one called 'Nellie'. Became the family's favourite. Built in 1918, registered as FX 7850 Fowler No 15319 with a 3-speed, 4-shaft engine. At first, she did work for the War Department, before her quarry days on Portland in 1921. Then, of course, we purchased her from the quarry in about 1931. The day she had to be collected from the quarry, 'Nellie' was in the bottom of a very steep quarry pit, and although she was a reasonable size, 7 n h p, they told James (Uncle Dick), "You have bought an engine you can't get out. She will never pull, it's too steep" (well of course she did, but only just.)

Little did 'Nellie' know here, the proud little showman's she was to become.
(Courtesy of Portland Steam Rally).

The Birth Of A Queen

So now, *'Nellie'* had to be converted to a showman's engine.

I must set the record straight now. It is written that Eddisons of Dorchester converted *'Nellie'* to a showman's engine, but this is NOT exactly true. Eddisons, did supply all the parts for the conversion to a showman's specification. The story of the conversion/building of her as a showman's, I was told many times by our uncle Tom Townsend. He and Uncle Dick spent all one winter converting her to a showman's, here in our village. *'Nellie'* was parked on Tidmoor Farm on Chickerell Road, which belonged to a Mr Harry Andrews, and Harry supplied the cups of cocoa while the men worked on the engine. Dick (the eldest) being the fine painter of the family, he painted her with gold lining.

Therefore, *'Nellie'* with a new canopy, dynamo and polished brass, and in our livery colours of maroon with gold lining, was now looking like a proud showman's engine. All she needed was a name to match.

'Queen Mary' at North Curry 1939
(reproduced by kind permission of the Surrey History Centre).

The family tended to name their transport after ships, and this engine was no exception. Tom chose the cruise liner called the 'Queen Mary', and as it happens he had a bottle of milk stout in his hand at the time, so he smashed it against *'Nellie's'* back wheel and said "there you are I name you 'QUEEN MARY'." So that is how our 'Queen' was born. And she still exists to day.

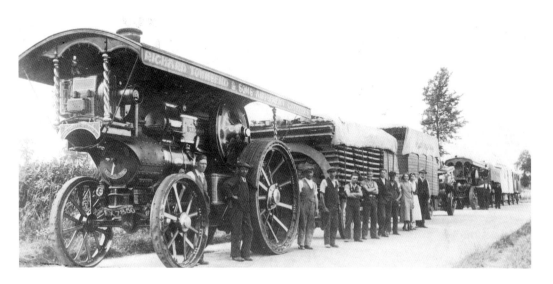

The family line up, with the 'Queen' towing.

In about 1933 they decided to have all her brass work chromed, including her wheel caps, which were so highly polished, that a lady could see her face perfectly, in them and could adjust her make up, (as one told me she actually did). The company that carried out the chrome work was Pender Plate in Poole.

However, the family agreed, the *'Queen'* had lost her looks, and she was not right, so they had all the chrome removed and had her brass put back as before.

What She Needed

It is thought she weighs about 18 tons and her water tanks hold about 350 gallons.

When she was pulling a big load, the water tanks would take her about 20 miles before the next fill up, which would be from a river or a spring. Yes, the family knew where every spring and river was for at least a 50-mile radius of Weymouth.

Her coalbunker would hold about 8cwt of coal.

The speed limit when on open roads was about 12 m.p.h.

But how they knew what speed they were doing, I don't know, as there was no Speedo.

Before attempting to go down hill, they would have to stop at the top of the hill in order to put her in a low gear first. Then when on level road again, stop, and change gear again. (No wonder travel was so slow.)

And of course, there was supposed to be the spark catcher on top of the chimney, which they were always being told off about, as they never had one, for a while. The police would stop them and make them put a bucket on top the chimney, which was a waste of time, as when the engine pulled away, the bucket would fly off.

The sparks would sometimes cause small fires along the grass verge, so one of the men had to jump off the engine, and stamp out the fire, then, of course, he would have to run and catch up with the engine again.

Supplying The Power At Night

The Gallopers had there own steam engine, in the centre of the ride itself, in order to keep it moving. Therefore, at first life was easy for the *'Queen Mary'*.

For the first three years, the *'Queen'* was only used for the towing on the road, plus supplying a little power for the lights at night. When other show families travelled with them, they also would draw power from this engine for the lights on their stalls, and at the end of the week, they would pay Richard a few pennies for this power.

It was not until 1935, when the Gallopers were sold, that the *'Queen'* had to really work hard, as not only did she have to tow on the road, but also now supply the power at night for their new Ark/ride (See Chapter Seven) which needed 110 volt power, which the *'Queen'* supplied through her 300 amp Newton dynamo (which is still on her today).

She would have to work hard, and would still use as much coal and water as if she was towing. When the Ark was turned on, you could hear the *'Queen'* loudly bark, as the ride pulled away gaining speed.

On such as a Saturday, the fair would open at 12 o'clock, and then close for about a hour at tea time. By 5 o'clock the fire box would be full of clinker, and would need emptying before the start of the evening.

In order to keep steam up, first they would top her boiler up with cold water to cool her, then quickly shovel out clinker from the firebox until empty, then throw in some sticks and a piece of paraffin rag, which would fire her up again. Very little pressure was lost, and she would be ready again, for when they opened at 6 o'clock.

When the day was over and it was time to close, only then they would climb upon her canopy to put an old milk churn lid on top of her chimney so to stop the fire drawing.

The new Ark she now had to run, taken 1935.

Her wire winch rope was about 50 yards long, and was once used when a tree was dangerously leaning over a house at Long Bredy, and the family were asked, if they would winch the tree away from the house.

Mr Denny Cave who knew the 'Queen Mary' well.
Originally, the wheels were also in red.

Denny, a cousin of the family, spent many years with us. He said that as a young man while they were open at Winfrith, a storm was brewing and Tom told him to dig a hole behind the *'Queen Mary'*, and bury one end of the chain that they always had attached to her back coupling, This was just in case the *'Queen'* was struck by lightning. If she was not earthed, and they were open at the time, the dynamo on the engine would be damaged (also, this could have killed Denny).

More about the *'Queen'* and her war days and the coal shortage in Chapter Eight.

When the family bought their first lorry (the Scammell) in 1946, the *'Queen Mary'* was not sold immediately, but worked alongside their first lorry for two years. This was a chain-drive Scammell, which you will read more about in Chapter Eleven, so the *'Queen'* did not retire until 1948. Then she stood in the yard in Putton Lane, covered up before she was sold on to a Mr Coombes in 1950, then a Mr Salmon owned her, then eventually Mr Cook, who has maintained her well. Whenever we look at her today, we still feel proud of her.

CHAPTER 6

1933 – Our Yard

In 1933 Kate decided that she no longer wanted to spend winters on someone else's land, and apparently said "I want somewhere for my children". So Kate found she was able to buy a turnip field, called Queen's Meadow in Putton Lane, in the village of Chickerell, near Weymouth.

The field was long and narrow with one gate and was about one acre. The cost was about £100. In 1933, that was a lot of money to them (but it was worth it, as five generations have lived here to this day).

The first winter they had to live with the mud, as the turnips had been pulled, leaving a ploughed field.

They also purchased some large chicken sheds to use as work/paint sheds for the Gallopers, as there were two fine painters in the family now, James (Uncle Dick) and Albert (Uncle Pat), both doing the paint work on the Gallopers ready for the following summer.

But there were no sheds for the traction engines, so all the water would be drained from their tanks, and then they would be covered completely in canvas, then rope would be wrapped around and around tightly to keep the winter elements at bay, and only in the spring would they be unwrapped ready for the coming season.

It was so muddy in the field during the winter when it had rained, that next they bought Portland stone, to use as a base stone.

Then they bought 1000's of red bricks from the Chickerell brickyard, these were delivered by cart, then the bricks were neatly and tightly laid on top of the stone, creating a brick road down through the centre of the long field. Then they stoked up the *'Queen Mary'*, and she was driven over the bricks so to press them firmly down (and to this day, there are still some of those bricks in place).

As Richard still had a pony and trap, they also built a small-galvanised shed as a stable for the horse.

During the Second World War, Weymouth, saw many dog fights in the skies, as our planes tried to protect the coast.

Then in 1941, it is believed a tracer bullet went through the roof of the stable during one of the dog fights.

The bullet landed in a big cloth/canvas tilt that had been hanging up inside the stable. (They would some times hang the top tilts from the ride, high in the roof to keep dry). The tracer bullet smouldered in the tilt for some time afterwards. Consequently, that day the stable caught fire. It was daytime, and only the women were in the yard at the time, so they sent for the men, who were cutting timber in Rempston woods. By the time the men arrived home, it was too late as the fire destroyed the stable… Thankfully, there was no horse in the stable, and no one was hurt.

Being wartime, and Kate being a shrewd lady, who had already been through one war, she knew prizes for the stalls would be in short supply during wartime.

Therefore, she bought tea chests full of such things as glass, and chalk figurines, as you would win on a fair ground in the 1940s. Unfortunately, all the tea chests were stored in the stable, so all the prizes were also destroyed in the stable fire.

They resorted to giving packs of 5 Woodbine cigarettes as a prize instead. Also, they would collect glass jars, and fill them with such as bath salts. Also, Woolworth stores were good for supplying prizes such as glass tumblers.

The stable was soon rebuilt, using blocks this time, and it is still there to this day…

The Near Miss

The yard was never actually bombed during the war, but did have a near miss one night, when the family heard a bomb whistle as it went close overhead. They thought this was it for them; however, the bomb landed on the farm next door at the end of the yard.

The next morning, the horse that belonged to the farmer in the next field, was found dead, he had been stood, but the shock of the blast made him go down on his knees, and that is how the horse was found, with his head lowered, but he was still upright. Also, when the farmer opened the barn door, every animal was dead, and did not have a single mark or cut on them. However, there was a cockerel that would roam freely from the farm to our yard, and the blast blew all his feathers off, so he looked as if he had been plucked. Apart from this he was ok, just bald and still roaming around.

Thankfully none of my family were hurt, the only casualty we had in the yard from the blast, was Uncle Tom's little puppy who was killed.

Now Taking Shape

It was not until the late 1940s that the yard really started to take shape, when the family started to have <u>wooden</u> chalet/kitchens built next to the trailers so in the winter time, we would spend the daytime in the chalets, for cooking and eating. We only used the trailers for sleeping at night. Also, now we had the chalets, and TV came along in the 1950s, we had the added luxury of television.

But I can tell you, it was hell when we had to pull out in the spring to start travelling again, and leave the TV behind. (This was before the battery TV was even thought of, and the only power we had in the summer was 110 volts, for the rides.) Therefore, it was strictly television in the wintertime only. Also now we were away from the yard and the electricity, it was back to the calor gas lights again and having to sit directly under the light in order to read anything. I can remember I liked the smell of a newly lit mantle, and how warm and cosy the trailer would be, with the small coal fire, whilst the evening entertainment was listening to the radio.

Back to the yard

In 1959 the big sheds were built, so the lorries and rides went under cover in the wintertime. The sheds are still there today, and I can remember my mother telling me "In 1959 we pulled out in the spring as usual, and we were away all summer open, and when we came back after Portland Fair, there they were all finished."

Then in the early 1960s, the first of the three family Bungalows started to appear. Therefore, the wooden chalet kitchens disappeared.

So that turnip field that Kate bought back in 1933, later became known as Townsend's Winter Quarters.

This was taken in the 1970s.

CHAPTER 7

1935 – They Bought An Ark

Taken on Weymouth Beach 1953 for Queen's Coronation.

The Ark (pictured above) replaced the Gallopers in 1934. It must have been one hell of a decision the family had to make to sell the Gallopers, as they had seen them through so much, but it was a matter of coming to terms with the fact that they had to move with the times to survive, and the public wanted new faster rides.

Someone happened to have a Noah's Ark for sale so Richard, Dick and Tom went to look at it. They were too late, as when they arrived, it had just been sold. (Uncle Tom told me "It was just as well, because what we ended up with in the end was far better".) They had to decide what to do next, and the decision was to go straight to the ride manufacturers Lakin & Co based at Streatham in London, to see if they could buy a new one. I asked my uncle what it was like when they arrived, he said "There were wooden animals all over the place, and it was a big open yard and all the men were building an Ark for someone else. We went there and ordered ours in the December, and it was ready for the spring, just right for the summer season."

The Ark was 42ft in diameter, with two or three animals on each platform section. There were 18 platforms altogether. Later on two of the platforms, the animals were removed and had chariots added.

The total cost of having the new Ark built was £1,025.

In order to try the new machine out, they built the Ark up here in the yard in Putton Lane and for one whole day only, all the village children could come for as many free rides as they liked before the family pulled out for the summer season.

Richard seen here with Jill (the 4th generation).

The front top rounding boards did not come with the ride when it was new, but were bought from another showman (Smarts). The boards were blank and were finally fitted on the ride during the war in 1944, while the family were open at Fair Fields Dorchester, (the market car park). The boards had to have new irons fitted in order to fit them to the ride. The boards were finally painted with the motor bikes, as they are in the picture on the previous page, by Mr Biles from Bridport who also did much of the sign writing on the lorry doors.

The bottom shutters/boards over the years had four different patterns of paintwork on them. When new, there were jungle scenes with tigers, then in later years scenes of Scotland, the lastly a pattern/design was painted on by James (Uncle Dick).

The centre truck had hard wheels when new, but they changed them for tyre wheels later.

Original Animals On The Outside Of The Ark

In 1963, twenty-nine years after they first bought the ride, the family updated the ride a little by removing the outside row of animals, and replacing them with wooden motor bikes, which the family bought from another showman, Bernard Cole at Southampton.

The bikes were stripped and repainted by Uncle Dick, Pat, and cousin Paddy. A little chrome work was also done on them. Also in 1963 they opened for the first time at what was to become one of their busiest places, Weymouth Carnival. This was also the first place the newly decorated motor bikes were used.

Sadly this same year just a few days after Weymouth Carnival, Kate and Richards first born James, (Uncle Dick) at the age of 64 passed away while they were at Sherborne for the carnival. Coincidently, James' grandfather William Townsend (Chapter One) also died at Sherborne in 1912.

Did You Know?

Many other showmen cut and altered their Ark's by turning them into Waltzers, which in the 60s was the modern ride to have. This meant replacing the animals with Waltzer cars, and they also would lower the machine by cutting the top down.

When our Ark was sold and finally left the family in 1989, it was one of only a few still in its original condition. More on the ark and the war in Chapter Eight.

With Compliments from

R. TOWNSEND & Sons

Fair Field.

This Card entitles Bearer to

ONE FREE RIDE ON THE
NOAH'S ARK OR SWINGS.

SCHOOL CHILDREN ONLY.

(Courtesy of Mr R Spooner)

CHAPTER 8

1940 – The Second War

3rd September 1939, war was declared. The family at the time were open at Mere in Wiltshire. The police came to the fair ground, and told them that now we were at war they were to return home to Weymouth, as the roads had to be kept clear for the Army. This therefore, is what they did.

However, it was what they called a 'phoney war.' The Government was preparing for war, and nothing happened for several months, so the family lost the end of the season, what we call 'the back end run', which is mostly carnivals.

The Government did not need to requisition their traction engines, as they did in World War one, as steam power now was too slow for the Government. Therefore, Richard was able to keep the engines.

However, there were no fairs open for the first three years of the war. So all the family had was timberwork (which you will see in the next chapter).

It was not until 1943 that they actually opened again for business.

It was in 1943 that the war was starting to take its toll on the population. Families before the war would spend their holidays at the seaside, but now the beaches were part of the British defence system, had barbed wired strewn along them, so it was impossible to go in the sea or even on the beach. Even the small children's Round-a-bout on the beach (Chapter Four) could not open.

Therefore, in 1943 the Government came up with the Holidays at Home idea having decided the nation needed cheering up. They approached fair ground families offering them the chance to open once again.

You have probably presumed that all the family were together during the war.

Well, only Richard, Kate and their daughters Hilda, and Doris were travelling, and, of course the men that were working for them as well. They travelled with the Ark, swinging boats, and the small hand-turned children's ride (Juvenile) and stalls.

Being wartime coconuts were not available so there was no coconut shy, instead it was 'touch-em's' (knock the pegs down).

The prizes were packs of 5 Woodbine cigarettes, or a drinking glass or jar full of bath salts. This is all they had, as remember (in Chapter Six Our Yard) how the stable burnt down and all the swag was also burnt.

Not that the family did much travelling the first year, in fact they only opened at 5 different places in total throughout the year, stopping for a number of weeks at each one.

There were wartime restrictions on lighting, and no bright lights were allowed on fair grounds. For example, on the Ark, which had 18 platform sections to make up its 42ft diameter, all they were allowed were 4 large light bulbs, we called them 300s; they were the same shape as your average house light bulb, but 4 times larger in actual size. Then they had to be painted black leaving a round circle on the bottom of the bulb clear, so only a small beam of light would shine down in order for the money takers to see the coins. However, for some reason these bulbs would not last long and it was presumed the paint was the cause, as the bulb must have been over heating? So they started to use nothing but blue lights from then on, but they gave little light and the ride looked dull. What did help matters was that the government put all the clocks forward by 2 hrs, so it did not get very dark until late, in fact I am told some nights it was still light when they closed, yet it was 10:00pm.

I have been told it was a lovely feeling, when the war was over and for the first time seeing the Ark with bright lights again.

The family's first place to open in 1943 was Salisbury, in the Victoria Park, for 6 weeks. Also there were Henry Chipperfields Galloper's. However, as this was the first time they had opened since the war started, they had no coal for the 'Queen Mary'. They ordered coal from the local train station, however no delivery came. So for several consecutive days they continued to reorder. Then when they gave up hope of getting a delivery, suddenly it finally came, but each order they had placed for the last several days all came at once, all 15 Tons of it, so now they had a glut of coal, some had to be bagged up and taken to the yard in Weymouth.

When they finally opened that day, it was worth the wait, as the people came in their hundreds, the Ark was riding full, every ride all day.

From then on wherever there was an Army camp, Richard would be open close by, places such as Salisbury, Blandford, Wareham, Shaftesbury, behind the Bee Hive pub at Wimborne and, of course, Dorchester. When the soldiers were sent away to fight and business went quiet, the family would then move on to the next camp.

Whilst open at Blandford the river burst its banks, and as they were pulling the Ark down, it was surrounded by 2ft of water and as they lifted parts of the ride up from the ground, the wood blocks/packing used for levelling the ride floated away.

Up until now and before the war, they had only travelled and opened in the summer, but in 1943, for the first time, they opened all winter as well, in Dorchester, at Fairfield's (now the Market car park) they joined Herbert's Fair, which had already been open at Dorchester for a while.

They opened every night, but when the snow became 3ft deep it was too cold to open so they had the night off.

At Christmas there was a big party put on for the local children by the American soldiers. Next to the fair was a big Bofors gun, which was for shooting down enemy planes when they were trapped in the searchlights. This gun was so loud going off, that it was frightening. This is something thankfully, we will never see in our lifetime, but can only imagine the horrific sight this must have been next to a fair. When the air raid sirens sounded, they would have to keep a look out, just in case they were about to be bombed by the enemy planes, luckily this never happened when they were open.

Uncle Tom and Tommy Herbert whilst they were at Dorchester, were also buying and selling old cars, so there was the fair ground one side of the field and the car sales the other side. This can only be described as the showman's adaptability during a war. The family spent a lot of time open in Dorchester during the winter, so much so, that they were able to use a building within the market place for painting and repairing the Ark. However, they had to have everything cleared out of the building on Wednesdays, for the market, as it was used for selling fowl. This building still exists and it is now an auction room.

The family were open at Dorchester at the beginning of June 1944. Business went quiet, as the soldiers were being sent away, and the country prepared for what we now know as D Day. It was so quiet the family only opened at weekends.

Of course, throughout the war they still were using the traction engines. They managed to stockpile some coal in the yard at Weymouth for the *'Queen Mary'*, and *'Princess'*, but usually stations were very good at providing the coal.

When open during this busy time and supplying the power to the Ark, the *'Queen Mary'* would burn as much coal as if she was towing on the road, as when the Ark/ride was turned on, you could hear the *'Queen'* working hard as the ride pulled away.

However, this did cause problems with the music, (the old records being played in the pay box).

As when the Ark was turned on and pulled away, so the amp meter went down for just a few seconds on the *'Queen'*, therefore so did the speed of the music. It sounded so funny, that eventually they could not stand it any more, and fitted a small resistance, in a belly box of the truck, along with the record player, this cured the music problem.

While at Dorchester with Herbert's, the Herbert's engine *'Majestic's'* dynamo caught fire, so our *'Queen Mary'* was pulled beside their *'Majestic'*, and helped them out by running their ride and stalls as well, until the repairs were finished.

On our *'Queen'*, there had to be someone on the engine to keep her going during this busy time and for many years it was a cousin of ours, called Denny Cave (who I must thank for his help in compiling this information).

On Saturdays, they would open in the afternoon for business. By the end of the afternoon, the *'Queens'* firebox was full of clinker. So they would top her up with cold water to cool her, then they would shovel the hot clinker out in to a bucket, the shovel would become white-hot doing this, so then they would have to throw the shovel in a bucket of water as well. Then they quickly would throw some sticks and paraffin rag in the firebox to light her up again before she lost much steam.

When it was finally time to close at night, they would then climb up and put the old milk churn lid on her chimney to stop the fire drawing.

When the war ended in Japan on the 15th of August 1945 and it was V J Day, Kate and Richard were open on the Weymouth Marsh.

Despite the whole country having a jubilant celebration, the family still opened, but no one can remember if they were busy, or if people were in the mood for the fair ground. All I do know is Joe and cousin Denny went to the pub to celebrate like thousands of others did, but they got drunk, and slept through whilst the rest of the family were open. The next day, boy did they get a telling off…!

This is the little ride from the beach (Chapter Four Weymouth Sands) due to the Weymouth Wartime coastal defences, for a time this ride came off the beach and travelled. This was taken at Bere Regis in 1944.

Remember me mentioning in Chapter Three, that the next important family trade would be timber, well the next chapter will tell you what the men of the family were up to.

CHAPTER 9

Still 1940, But With Timber

In Chapter Three (Building a Business), I mentioned when living at Buckland Ripers, that the family were selling logs from a horse and cart in the winter months for a little extra money while the Gallopers were closed. Then when in 1933 Kate bought the yard in Putton Lane, the family continued selling the logs in the wintertime.

Therefore, by 1940, they had now been living in the yard in Putton Lane for seven years, and they were still cutting and selling the timber… World War Two had just started and wood would be needed for the war effort. My family must have approached the Government and offered their services, as all four sons, James, Tom, Pat and Joe, plus cousin Denny Cave, were hauling the trees out of local woods for the Forestry Commission. In-laws were also with them so there were actually seven members of the family away doing the timber.

They worked in 4 different woods at various times from 1940 to 1945 such as Rempston, Stourpaine, and Whitechurch, and finally Lulworth.

The family did not use the *'Queen Mary'* or *'Princess'* for the timber. The two engines were used again in 1943 when the rest of the family started to open again with the fair, travelling around the camps and opening at Dorchester.

Therefore, they acquired 2 Fodens Steam wagons, one of which was called *'Little Lady'*. A 4 n.h.p "D" Type tractor No 13444.Built 1924, weight 8 tons.

'Little Lady' Dorchester Rally 1960
She still exists today (Courtesy of Brian Burden).

The steam Fodens were needed for their winches. These were used to winch the felled trees up on the flat four-wheel timber carriage/trailer.

First, the Forestry Commission would decide which trees were to be cut down, by scratching a large cross on the tree.

Other people working for the Forestry Commission actually cut the trees down, so all my family had to do is haul the trees out (whole).

The largest of the trees came out of the Weld Estate at Lulworth. The girth of these trees could be anything up to 8 ft wide. A tree of that size could take a whole day to cut. After the tree had been felled, all the limbs would be sawn off and cut into cord wood. The main trunk of the tree would not be cut, but would be measured by the Forestry Commission. First the girth, then the length, so they could work out the cubic feet, which was noted down in a small book and a tag would be placed on the bottom of the tree. The Forestry needed to know this information, so they knew what to charge the sawmill, and the tree fellers were paid by the size of tree they had cut down.

Timber was needed to make items such as duckboards, rifle butts, parts for landing craft and coffins, to name just a few.

The smaller/thinner trees were used for such as telegraph poles. This was something this country needed at lot of, due to the bombing. From the Lulworth Estate small ash trees were also cut, and these were for making propellers for Spitfires.

First, we would pull the timber carriage alongside parallel with the fallen tree. Long timbers would be leant leading from the ground to up to the carriage.

Then wire rope would be wrapped around the tree leading to the winch. The tree would then be rolled upon the timber carriage.

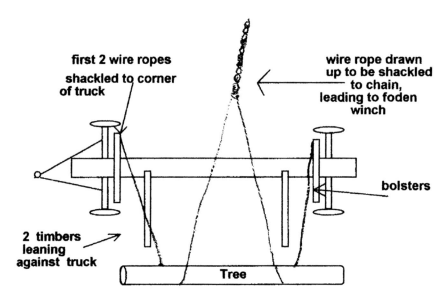

first 2 wire ropes shackled to corner of truck

wire rope drawn up to be shackled to chain, leading to foden winch

bolsters

2 timbers leaning against truck

Tree

Also at each end of the carriages, there was a bolster, which could hold an 8ft wide tree in place. The pole of the bolster would be pinned into place, stopping the tree from rolling off.

TREE PINNED IN PLACE BETWEEN BOLSTER

The Carriage/trailer was very cleverly made, as they were extendable so they could carry the longest or the shortest of trees.

Also, they bought 2 lorries, a petrol Leyland, (Hippo) and a petrol Bedford. The Bedford could have been an exchange, as a advert in the 'Commercial Motor' dated September 1940 Burrell compound *'steam tractor, in good condition suitable for any work, will exchange for good Bedford lorry. Apply R. Townsends'.*

The Bedford was used to transport the timber to the sawmills, Sydenhams in Poole. If Sydenhams had a glut of timber, they would ask them to stop delivering for a few days. However, the men would carry on dragging the trees out, and then stack them in a field ready to deliver later.

Whilst working in the forest, the men lived in an old 12 ft wagon and a 6ft by 8ft shed. All cooking was done on two Primus stoves and was mostly done by Uncle Pat.

There was a condition when working for the Forestry Commission, that the men were not allowed to return home to the fair ground for more then 48 hours a week, as only because they were doing a job of national importance, for the Forestry Commission, were they exempt from fighting.

When the men returned home at weekends, it would be to wherever the rest of the family were open with the Ark and stalls. Then they would collect a large hamper basket full of cooked meats and fruit pies, which Hilda had cooked for them to take back to the woods.

There were no fridges then so I am not sure how long the food would have lasted.

There were no shortages of meat in the forest, as they would snare rabbits and shoot pigeon. Pigeon eggs tasted good, so I am told.

Winters would be very hard, as they would work through all weathers, rain, snow and stopping for nothing. A bowl of water left on the sideboard in the old wagon has been known to freeze over and their wet trousers worn from the previous day, would be frozen stiff by morning.

Personal hygiene could be a problem, as the water tap would freeze up, and so a paraffin rag would be wrapped around the tap and set light to, and this would normally work. Hot water for washing in could be got from the steam Foden boiler, not that it would be very clean.

On D-Day 6th June 1944, the men watched our planes go over the Lulworth Estate for the invasion.

On V E day in May 1945, the men were still on the Weld Estate at Lulworth at the time, and work stopped immediately now the war was over.

Uncle Dick, Tom, Pat and Joe were released from their duties and returned home to travelling again. The family were open at Dorchester at the time.

When the war ended, the family continued with the timber during the winter, they were cutting trees at Fleet, near Weymouth. In the early 50's they found an ex-Army Mack lorry for sale. It had been working in an orchard in Somerset. They bought it to help drag out the timber (more on this lorry in Chapter 12). They continued in the winter months by buying a Bedford lorry and delivering bags of logs around the households in Weymouth. They did the house deliveries for about 28 years.

My dad Joe and Uncle Pat would leave the yard about 8.30, in the morning with the Bedford loaded up high with logs, and would return about 4 o'clock empty, then load the lorry up for the next morning. They would be out on the lorry five and half days a week and would only have Saturday afternoon off, as Sunday they would be in the big paint shed doing something to the rides, like painting and repairing them ready for the summer season. Then Monday morning it was back on the log lorry again. They also did large bags of nicky/kindle wood.

I can remember as a little girl, having to hold up the sack bags so my dad could fill them with the sticks of nicky/kindle wood. I hated doing it as my thumbs would be scratched by the sticks. When I was fed up in the yard with no one to play with, I would go in the stable and sit on a big tree log we used as a seat, with a smaller block in front of me and chop the nicky wood myself, through boredom. So yes, I was chopping from a young age and never cut myself once, but I was not allowed to split the logs until I was 12.

For many years you could buy bags of logs from the yard as well. The locals would wait until November, and when our sign was out by the gate, they knew we were back in business again, and would call in.

It was I who was the last member of the family to sell logs from the yard. After my mother's death in 1980, I decided the profit margin was too low, so I decided not to continue. After 50 years of the family doing timber, it was the end to an era in this family, but I never realised it at the time.

CHAPTER 10

1945 – The Boom

In Chapter Eight, I mentioned how the Government allowed the family to open again in 1943 as part of the Government's Holidays at Home idea, which they did, near such places as the Army camps at Salisbury, Blandford, and Wareham.

Most places they opened, they were busy, and so the family had been used to taking good money wherever they opened for the last two years of the War.

So now it's 1945 and the war is over.

Remember me mentioning the boom was yet to come, in Chapter Three? Well this was it.

For the last five years many things had been on ration, soldiers were being paid to fight, but there was little to spend their money on. There were very few luxuries to be had, food was short, and no holidays were taken, so some were able to save a little money. Then, when the war was declared over, both Herbert's and Townsend's pulled out of Dorchester and went to Bridport to open. Then they returned to Dorchester for the home-coming celebrations. The soldiers returned home to their loved ones, and they were all given demob money as well. Therefore, there was great celebration, and boy did they celebrate! Everyone decided to enjoy themselves by spending some of their money. There was little entertainment to chose from it was the cinema, the theatre or the fair.

Therefore, everywhere Townsend's opened they did well. One such place was Portland Fair. As usual at Portland Fair, there were other show families there with their big rides as well. At this particular busy time, there were so many people that the rides were riding full every time.

The punters stood just about anywhere they could on the ride itself, ready to jump on as soon as the ride slowed down.

The boom time really put all the showmen back on their feet.

The boom lasted for the next five years until the country got back to normal and luxuries became available again. Because money was now truly coming in, the family had to make the most of it, so they bought their next big ride in 1948 which was the brand new Super Car Dodgems (see Chapter Thirteen).

CHAPTER 11

1946 – Little Scammell

The Scammell CD45
(courtesy of the late Stuart Beaton collection).

We have progressed from the 1800s, when any fair ground ride relied on the horse for travelling until 1860 when in came the steam.

Therefore, until now the traction engines, *'Queen Mary'* and *'Princess'* had been supplying the power at night and, of course, towing every thing on the road by day. However when it came to the towing, the traction engine was just too slow.

So in 1946, they decided to retire the *'Princess'*, as they now could afford to have their first lorry for the travelling, a chain-drive Scammell. When the family paid for her, it was not entirely with the old £5 notes of the time. They travelled by train to collect her carrying suitcases full of half crowns and two shilling pieces as well, and that's how they paid for her. She had to be collected from Watford. However before a member of the family could leave the factory with her, they first had to drive on a practice pad, to show they were able to handle her on the road.

1946. Feeling proud with the new Scammell, with no body on her yet.

But in all honesty, they were not a good buy, and the showmen found this out when it was too late and they were not happy when the new Showtrac came out, which was far better.

They brought our little Scammell back to Dorchester, to the Fairfields car park, where they were open at the time. An Uncle (Marshal Herbert) drove her back, but it was such a bad experience he vowed never to drive her again. She was just a chassis cab when new, so we had to add the body to her. She was plain grey in colour, and came with her own toolbox that consisted of a spanner which fitted everything.

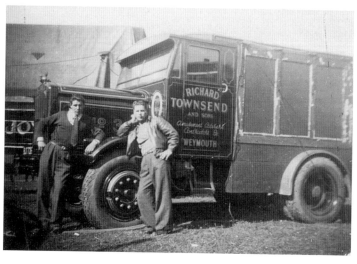

At first we had a lot of trouble with her fuel, only to discover that the fuel tank had rust in it. We contacted Watford, to tell them. The reason they gave was that they made so many fuel tanks, they were stood around for a while before being fitted. They did not supply a new one, instead cousin Denny managed to clean ours out, but gave himself dermatitis in doing so.

Ours being chain-driven. had two chains, one either side leading from the drive shaft, to the back axle.

Her top speed was about 20 m.p.h flat out down hill, which was not a great improvement on the traction engine *'Princess'*. Due to the size of the 2 sprockets, and the thick chains, she was able to tow up to 45 tons.

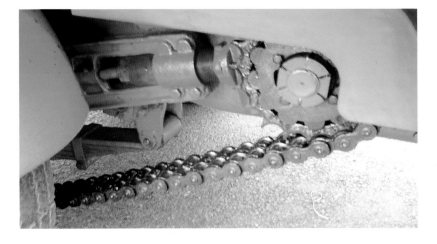

This picture is of a Scammell with a 19 teeth sprocket, so by law she could tow 45 Tons, 3 trailers, or up to 90 Feet.

When it came to her <u>engine reliability</u>, without a doubt she was the best and she rarely let us down, with a Diesel 6 LW Gardner engine of 102 h.p, doing about 10 miles to the gallon.

However the family still had to stop and fill up at streams every 20 miles, as they still had 'Queen Mary', because for two years both traction engine and Scammell worked alongside one another. So in 1946 the family were still buying coal for the 'Queen', and would now buy something called gas oil, for the Scammell, which was really diesel but with no tax, so it was cheaper to buy at only one shilling per gallon.

Then the Government wanted more tax, so red dye was added to some diesel, but lorries had to be run on white diesel, and the cost went up to half a crown a gallon.

The Scammell had many drawbacks

Here are just a few. When we were in a muddy field, she would always get stuck. She did not like soft ground at all, and had to be winched out many times.

Also, she was uncomfortable, as the seats were just wood with a thin layer of horse hair covered by leather. As Uncle Dick was short, his legs were not long enough to reach the pedals, so they put blocks on the pedals to make them higher up.

She had four gears, plus reverse. When changing from 3rd to 4th, as long as you remembered to double de-clutch, you were ok. She was very low geared; so much so you could pull away in top.

However, she had to almost stop in order to change into bottom gear before pulling a steep hill. There is one particular hill in Somerset, called Wynyard's Gap, that is known to be very steep and long, and towing two trucks it would take about 20 mins for her to pull it.

Why There Had To Be A Block Boy
Riding On The Open Truck Behind

For the first few years there was a young man called Ralph Castleman who would ride on the open truck that was being towed behind. His job was to take care of the brakes on the two trucks when they were either about to climb a hill or go down one.

Early 50s (courtesy of the Stuart Beaton collection).

When approaching the <u>top</u> of a hill, before she could go down it, Uncle Dick would give one toot on the horn.

This would tell the block boy to jump off the truck behind, while they were still moving (about 3 m.p.h). The boy would run down one side of the load and apply the brake handles on both trucks, then the Scammell would be put into bottom/ crawler gear.

The brakes on the trucks would be left on down over the hill, in order to hold back the two trucks, this would help prevent the weight, from pushing the Scammell forward, as the two trucks combine weight, was more then the Scammell.

When they were on level road again, two toots on the horn would the tell the block boy to let both the brake handle off again on both trucks.

When the boy had done this, he would then run <u>between</u> the back of the lorry and truck, (still moving), climb up on the high draw/tow bar, and sit back on the truck being towed. (Can you imagine what health and safety would say nowadays?)

By the time they had reach the bottom of the hill, the breaks on the truck was very hot, and smelling so too.

As she was only a small Scammell, there was also the risk of her being pulled backwards when going <u>up</u> hills.

Therefore, they had to make sure she was in bottom gear <u>before</u> starting to pull. They could not risk slowing to a stop, in order to change gear, ounce they were so far <u>up</u> a hill, as she could have been pulled backwards, by the combine weight of the two trucks.

However, the block boy always knew, there were blocks on the truck to quickly put behind the wheels if any thing like this should happen.

The Scammell breaks were transmission and could not be used much, as they would catch fire. So only when doing short stops, was the foot brake really used. When approaching a junction, it would reduce speed well in advance, and use very little foot brake.

After a few years, the block boy was no longer needed, as the drivers got to know the lorry/gear box well, and how steep the hills were around here and besides there was always a chap in the passenger seat to jump out if need be.

And don't forget the addition of air brakes were fitted in the late 50's.

Supplying The Power At Night

When we added the body on the back of her when new. Before the body could be fitted, a concrete ballast was put down in the floor, for <u>two</u> reasons, first to add weight to her, also to attach a steel runners on to, which then a dynamo was bolted to the runners, (the dynamo was to supply the power at night). The only thing we put in the back of the body, was a Phoenix 500 amps dynamo, which they drove the

Scammell to Bath to collect. It drove the Ark ride and lights when open. Which meant every new place we visited, the Scammell was driven on blocks to level her. Then as she was a chain drive, two of her chains were removed, and 2 thinner chains were led up from the driveshaft up inside the body to two 7 inch sprockets, one on each side of the dynamo.

Then she would be put in 4th gear, and would run continually at approx 1,000 revs, driving the dynamo in the back of her, the dynamo then running at 500 Revs.

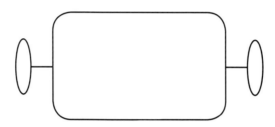

As I said earlier, when it came to her engine, she was the best. The dynamo had two wires leading to a switchboard, which had two more long cable wires leading to the Ark.

Remember me mentioning in Chapter Four (the Steam and our Queen) how the *'Queen Mary'* was named after a ship? well so was the Scammell.

Vanguard

In 1972, the Scammell went into retirement and remained under our sheds in the yard covered over for a few years. Until one of our other lorries let us down one year, so the Scammell came out of retirement for one summer only, then she was returned to the sheds again till she was finally sold to a dealer in 1989. Then she seamed to disappear. Remember the Scammell had been with us for 43 years, and we the 4th generation had grown up with her always being there, so we wondered what had happen to her?

So the family spread word that we were trying to trace her and for 13 years, she just went astray. Then in 2001, a Mr Mike Harris of London contacted us to say he had purchased her, so the family had finally found her again.

CHAPTER 12

1947 – Goodbye Steam, Hello Lorry

In 1946 the family had bought their first lorry the Scammell and they also still had the *'Queen Mary'* working alongside the Scammell.

In 1947, as WW2 had ended, the family discovered that the Army had surplus lorries, Macks to be precise. They were to have been shipped abroad, for use as tank recovery/transporters.

They were brought over here by the Americans, but when they returned home to the States after the war, they did not take the Macks home with them. Now the war had ended, they were still here unused. Soon after the war a lot of ex-Army surplus items came up for sale through auctions. The showmen attended many of these auctions, taking advantage of the bargains to be had.

Ours came up for sale at the Middle Wallop (Hampshire) Army Auctions.

The Mack which we successfully bid for was BTK 895. Being American, it was left hand drive and known as a Super 6.

(I remember Uncle Tom telling me "It had air horns. But when we went to collect it they were gone, we could buy them separately for £20 " (which we did). The Mack was like brand new, and still had the stickers on the windscreens and brown paper on the seats, with hardly any miles on the clock.

Two things happened in 1948. The family bought a new set of dodgems, and retired their last traction engine *'Queen Mary'*, So they finally said goodbye to steam. However just the Scammell on its own was not enough, so the Mack was the replacement for the *'Queen'*. We bought the Mack in 1947, and put her on the road in 1948.

The wheels were 1200/24, which we could not get the tyres for, so they were changed to 40/8. The cab was canvas with half doors.

The cab was rebuilt by Ron Berry a local carpenter in our village. As usual our transport was named after a ship and 'THE LEADER' was the chosen name for this one.

The Leader BTK 895, Blandford, June 1968.

You will notice the wheels were painted with white distemper paint. By this era, Townsends were renowned for all their equipment being well maintained and painted, and apparently white tyres were the fashion at the time, red being our main livery colour.

The lorry doors were letter painted by Mr Biles from Bridport.

With its original large 6 litre <u>petrol</u> engine, it would do about <u>3 miles</u> per gallon, but was renowned for always breaking down, usually with coil problems. Also it use to backfire a lot when going down hills.

However, one thing can be said for this one, when she got going, boy did she move. In fact whoever was driving her, was told don't hold her back let her go, or if not she will burn more petrol. Over the next 22 years, because she was so fast, all the lorries we had working alongside her, she would over take the lot, and always pulled into the next place first.

On the back of her was a chain block on a high arm, which was for lifting the Ark centre truck, in order to remove the wheels from beneath it when building up.

BTK 895 'The Leader' in 1973. Still exists as far as we know.

The family bought two generators from another showman, Edwards at Basingstoke. These generators with 6LW Gardner engines, were ex-minesweeper engines, using 1 gallon of red diesel per hour. In the 1950s one of these generators was put on the back of *'The Leader'* to power the dodgems at night. The second generator stood in the yard for a while.

(Courtesy of Mr G Smart)   *Using the chain block to lift Ark centre.*

Garth The Second Mack

Although the war was over, the family were still doing timber, by cutting trees in the winter, to sell on themselves as logs. They decided they wanted another Mack to help with the timber business and in the early 50s the family found another Mack for sale at Hinton St George, Somerset, working in an orchard.

This one also had a new cab built by Mr Berry and was eventually withdrawn from the timberwork in the late 50s. It then started to travel alongside the other Mack. So now it was one Scammell and two Macks on the road travelling.

DFX 98, July 1967, named 'GARTH' and was eventually scrapped.

The original petrol engine was replaced with a <u>smaller diesel</u> one, which improved the mileage, it would now do about 8 miles per gallon. The Gardner engine came out of an old Scammell that years beforehand had belonged to another showman, Anderton and Rowland's.

But it was not successful, it was much slower, now the petrol engine had been replaced with a diesel, There is a particular long, steep hill in Somerset, called Wynyard's Gap that I have mentioned before. The Scammell would take about 20 mins to pull it with the loads behind; however, the diesel Mack would take 45 mins, which was not much better than the traction engine had been, as when she was put in crawler gear she hardly moved. In fact, she was so slow, that cousin

Jimmy got out of the cab when she was still moving, he would then go in the pub, which is half way up the hill and have a quick shandy, then catch up with *'Garth'* and clime back in the cab and she was moving through out the whole process.

So for 22 years, it was Scammell and Mack, as our main lorries, plus one or two others which joined along the way, but that's another story.

The Scammell was retired in 1972, and therefore we no longer had her dynamo for the power when open. By now the family had put the second generator (from the yard), on the back of the second Mack (GARTH). Later the family made up two more generators themselves, with a Maudsley dynamo on one and on the second one they used the dynamo off the *'Queen Mary'*. These two generators were also put on the back of the Macks. So now both Macks had two generators on the back, one on each being kept as a spare/back up. Our motto was "You can never have too much power". That is one situation my family never had, a ride closed through lack of power, now having 4 generators altogether. Now over 45 years later, although the *'Queen Mary'* is not in our ownership, the original dynamo has been returned to her.

In February 1972, when the national power strikes were on, the Weymouth GPO sorting office was having a problem, as the lights would go out when the postmen were trying to sort the letters in order to deliver them.

Therefore, they approached my family and asked if they could hire the generators while the strikes were on. As it was now wintertime and the generators were not needed for opening, one of the Macks went to the post office yard in Weymouth. Of course as our generators were 110 power (for the rides) so the main post office shop and sorting office had to have our lamp battens on the ceiling as well.

I was only 13 at the time, and not knowing of the arrangement with the family, that our 2 generators were in the post office back yard, you can imagine the look on my face, when I visited the post office, only to look up, and see the lamp battens off our ride on the ceiling!

We Had "C Licences"

As a child I can remember that apart from the road tax disc, there were "C licences" in the lorry windows. There were 3 types of disc available:

'A', to carry anything, anywhere.

'B', only within a certain radius.

'C', haul your own goods only.

Hence we had to have the 'C '.

The Lorries Later To Follow

Albion Caledonian XAM 14, and was a ex-tanker.
We converted from 8 wheeler to 6-wheel tractor.

Atkinson 277 NKL, 1973.   *466 RKO, taken 1987.*
Ex Furnell & Sons, Parkstone.

CHAPTER 13

1948 – DODGEMS

In 1948 as the family had been taking good money throughout the boom years (Chapter Ten) so they took delivery of the new Super Car Dodgems. They opened for the first time at Sherborne for the carnival.

At the time, my mum and dad were <u>courting</u> and mum only lived 3 miles from Sherborne. One day my dad said he could not see her the following night, as they were open with their new Dodgems, so my mum being curious, caught the bus to Sherborne to see what these new Dodgems were like. I remember her telling me "When I arrived your dad was sat in the pay box, and your Uncle Tom and Uncle Pat were pushing the cars around the track with the people in them".

The new Dodgems did not come with a top tilt when new, and on their first night open, it rained. The rain on the track affected the contact of the car wheels on the metal plates/track, so the first night did not go well.

Afterwards, another showman, Bernard Hill loaned them his spare tilt, while the family had one made. They also did not come with any transport, so two flat trucks were made by Sampson's of Dorchester.

The Dodgem floor/track was 60ft by 40ft in diameter and consisted of 76 plates, and around them 22 upright/pillars to hold the top. The ride was only altered once. That was by cutting/lowering the top by 6 inches, I was told this was because they swayed in the wind.

During the time we had them, they had one complete new set of 76 floor plates, which came while they were open at Swanage.

In 1953, the Dodgems were built on Weymouth sands along with the Ark, for the Queen's coronation. This was not one of the family's better ideas, as not only did they not take much money, but also sand got into the small Dodgem motors, which of course are inside every car. For some time afterwards a few motors every week had to be sent away to be cleaned of sand (only a few at a time could be sent, as they were open every week at other carnivals). Therefore, each week they opened they were a few cars missing, which meant loss of money and they vowed never to take the Dodgems on the sands again. The closest they ever came to sand again was in 1963, when in the August each year they would open on Weymouth Esplanade for the Weymouth Carnival.

Cousins Bernard and Denny in The Victory car.

In 1960 it was decided to have the cars sprayed and Mr Randall at Sutton Poyntz, did the cars for us. However, he had a few problems. He removed all the little bonnets and sprayed them in three different colours, but when replacing them on the cars, each bonnet would not fit any car, as each body was slightly different in size. Trying to match the bonnet colour to the rest of the car proved difficult, and some had to be re-sprayed.

Mr Randall's daughter Suzy would help the family when they were open at Bowleaze Cove, here in Weymouth. Every Friday she would stand in the river that ran alongside the fair and get buckets of water to wash the Dodgem floor/plates. She hated doing this as the river was full of eels and they would be wriggling around her feet as she collected the water.

The water would be thrown across the track, then cleaned off with a rubber squeegie. This was to clean off any carbon on the track.

Portland Fair.

The top rounding boards did not come with the ride when new, so the family bought them in the 60s from a showman called Teddy Morley. All we did was change the lettering to our name.

THE FLOOD

In July 1955 whilst open at Bowleaze Cove and next to the sea, a small river called The Jordan, which ran only yards away, burst its banks.

As there were holiday caravans close by, the flood not only made the holiday caravans float, including all their gas cylinders, but also it flooded the fair.

The dodgem floor/plates slightly lifted with the water and believe me each plate was heavy; it takes two strong men to lift one.

The wooden bridge the punters would have to cross in order to get to the fair was washed away, so the Army came and built a temporary Bailey Bridge.

Uncle Pat's Hoopla was washed out to sea and never seen again. However the game, rings and blocks that were in it floated, and were all washed up with tide about a mile away on Weymouth beach - coincidentally right where the other part of the family business was, the Swings and Round-a-bout on Weymouth sands (Chapter Seven) so my Uncle Frank collected all the rings and blocks, and sent

them back to the family at Bowleaze, so Uncle Pat got a another hoopla to put them in. The mud was so bad after the flooding they could not open for few days until it was cleared.

Our dodgem track/plates were made of alloy, therefore, they were always dark grey with alloy dust. I can remember my mother telling me how as a child, one morning she dressed me in an all white brand new outfit, apparently I looked beautiful in my little white pleated skirt. Then I made my way to the Dodgem Track, and yes, the clothes were ruined, I came home black. My mum said she had learned never to put me in white again.

Each year at Sherborne, the Carnival Queen would be crowned on the fair ground. They would use one of our flat platform trucks, putting a big blue cover over it, so that it looked like a nice stage. However, one year it rained, so they put some kitchen chairs in a line in the centre of the dodgem track, and crowned her there. Apparently, her dress and the attendant dresses were black all around the bottom by the time they had finished. The alloy dust would very rarely wash out.

As a child, I liked playing with money. I can remember sitting in the pay box, on my Uncle Tom's lap while we were open. He would allow me to stack the half crowns and two-shilling pieces that the money takers had put on the counter in front of us, but always I would end up dropping some money on the floor, so then my Uncle would shout and throw me out the pay box.

Call it a silly thing to remember, but all travellers will have childhood memories, that they will look back on and bring a smile to their face later in life, and what a carefree life it was too.

THIS PAY BOX WAS ALWAYS THE ORIGINAL FROM NEW.

1974

Bakers Ground, Portland
(Courtesy of Mr Andy White).

Wool Street Fair 1972.

DON'T FORGET . . .

WOOL FAIR

FRIDAY and SATURDAY
(May 15 and 16)

On the VILLAGE GREEN

DODGEMS, CHILDREN'S ROUNDABOUT
NOAH'S ARK, SIDESHOWS, REFRESHMENTS
Open Friday, 6.30 p.m.; Saturday 2.30 p.m.

We Had A Tractor

Over a number of years, we kept a tractor, a Ford D Major. When we did the back end run of carnivals, most years there would be wet weather due to the time of year (in late summer).

Of course, we had the mud as well, so we and the other showman travelling with us would get stuck, and needed to be dragged out the fields. Therefore, we had a tractor with a very good winch. We transported the tractor around with us on a flat four-wheel trailer. We always made sure the showmen that were with us were not stranded in the fields. This tractor was also used to help get the small Round-a-bout centre truck on the beach (Chapter Four).

(Courtesy of Mr N Haime)

Did You Know?

Have you ever considered how life was for the woman on the road?

I know that in the beginning of this book in 1871, Ann and William were living in a small wagon and cooking was done outside on a fire. It was a very cold life. Life was like that for a number of years.

Then in the 1930s, small square tents were built next to the trailers, for doing such as the washing, and cooking. All water had to be carried, and then boiled up on a primus. as there was no calor gas at this time.

When at some villages, Kate would ask around and find a local woman to do the washing, so each day a bundle of clothes would be delivered to a woman's house and a clean lot would be collected. In fact, when my mum and dad were courting in 1946, he would walk her home with a bundle of dirty washing under his arm, as my other gran did washing for Kate whilst they were open at Milborne Port. However, I am not sure what the women were paid in the village by the family for this service.

Then in the 1940s, the tents disappeared, as more modern trailers came along, with first, a fire/cooking range, then later the calor gas cooker. So now cooking was done inside, but the washing was still done outside in an old bath with a scrubbing board. The amount of water you had for this depended on how far it had to be carried. Sometimes you had to make it last, as there could be a restriction, like you could only have water from a tap at a certain time.

I can remember putting buckets at each corner of our trailer in order to catch rainwater, as it meant less water we had to carry for doing the washing. Later laundrettes came along, so in some towns we were lucky. We could not have washing machines ourselves, as the concept of plumbing in the ever-moving trailers was not thought of until the 1980s. Then of course, there is living with the mud. All showmen spend so much of the year in fields; the women have become experts at keeping mud under control inside and accept mud as an unfortunate part of life.

The post. You certainly do not get on a daily basis, we had our letters redirected by an auntie who knew where we were each week.

The showmen's contact before the mobile phone was limited but they managed. As there are no loft spaces in trailers, sentimental items are kept to a minimum. Someone asked me what it was like when we were about to go on the road. All the china in cabinets would be wrapped in towels or laid between blankets on the bed. Kitchen cupboards had to be tied shut, and we stood something in front of the doors to stop food or crockery from falling out. All washing up had to be done.

Both water cans would be filled before leaving the field, as you did not know if water would be available at the next place.

If you ask me what a woman had to be in this life, I would say a wife, mother, housekeeper, earner, business partner, secretary, and most of all tolerant.

The man is the, earner, driver, painter, repairer in all aspects, and never forgetting his wife, who will be beside him through everything. That is probably why in this business there are few divorces, as there has to be communication, and the struggle of building a business together makes a stronger marriage.

CHAPTER 14

1953 – Bakers Ground

The <u>custom</u> fair on the Island of Portland, was always held 5th & 6th November, and has been held at the bottom of the Island, in Chiswell for many years.

Richard had been attending Portland Fair for many years as a young man.

Then in the late 1940s, he found a piece of land called Bakers Ground, situated right in the centre of Chiswell. The land was a repossession by the Midland Bank and the land was available to rent from the bank. It was a prime spot to open for the Portland Fair.

Therefore, Richard for a few years rented Bakers Ground. He would open two weeks prior to the fair, then pull the Ark down and move it further up in Chiswell and build it up in the street for the actual two Fair days, leaving the small stalls and someone else's ride in Bakers Ground on their own. Then in later years, the Ark was not moved for the fair days, but stayed in Bakers Ground.

In about 1953, Richard bought the land from the Bank.

Originally the land belonged to the church, then someone called Baker owned it and it was always known as Bakers Ground after that, no matter who owned it.

You will note from the picture that there were three gates. this was ideal, as we would open all three, so the punters could walk from the street fair to us. It was an unusual situation, the street was rented from the local council by another show family, and as we owned Bakers Ground, we were a fair within a fair. However, we always opened a few days prior to the fair itself.

Bakers Ground was owned by three generations of my family, the last being two cousins, and myself. Then in 2001 we finally decided to sell.

Two Other Rides

In the early 50s, the family bought a small wheel. It was not a children's size (Juvenile) and not your average size fair ground wheel, but it was in-between. It would only hold one adult and one child in each car. However this ride was not very good, because if there was too much weight in a car, the ride would only take the riders so far up, and refuse to take them all the way around. This must have been embarrassing for whoever was looking after the ride. In the 60s, the ride was sold.

Portland November 1972.

In 1967, the family bought an Octopus ride, from Jones Brothers. Whilst we had this ride, a Leyland (Hippo) was used for its transport. We owned the ride until 1977, when we sold it to Charles Coles. We did not use this ride much. I have since been told it was scrapped in 2004.

*Blandford, 1972 the Leyland now gone, and the last year for the Scammell.
Seen here towing the Octopus.*

CHAPTER 15

1950 -1960 Passed Away

In Chapter Three Richard and Kate met when Richard was open with his father behind The Quicksilver Mail pub in Yeovil.

Now 54 years later in 1950, Kate passed away in her sleep, here in the yard, in Putton Lane.

As a pretty young Sunday school teacher, and landlord's daughter, Kate Force had met Richard Townsend, whom she married. They had 6 children, built a business surrounded by their children, and went through all the hardships of life together. They survived two World Wars, and the Depression, and still came out on top. They were known and respected by many people; and together they built a life that that shaped the generations to come.

A quote from the World's Fair.

The Perfect Partnership

Mrs Townsend left the more active running of the Round-a-bouts to her husband, and tended to the business and books side of the business. It was the perfect partnership between husband and wife.

Ten Years Later 1960

For about five weeks every year July to August, we would open in a field situated in the centre of holiday camps here in Weymouth. During one such year 1960, Richard being 94 years old was frail, and had not been well, and consequently in August 1960, ten years after Kate, Richard also passed away. Because the family were not far away from the yard at Chickerell, they laid Richard out in his wagon, then towed the wagon out of the fair ground, and took it to the yard in Putton Lane, so his funeral cortege was led from the yard.

A Quote From The World's Fair Paper

By Jim Lewis
August 20th 1960.

On hearing over the wireless of the death of Mr Richard Townsend, I went to Weymouth to express my sympathy and to see if I could be of any service to the family of this grand old gentleman.

Mr Townsend first became ill at Chard (Somerset) May fair. At 94, he must have been one of the oldest members of the Showmans' Guild, if not the oldest. I have had the privilege of knowing Mr Townsend and his family for 22 years; I have been particularly interested in how they quietly go about their business, and at no time seeking the limelight.

The last time I had the pleasure of talking to Mr Townsend was at Portland Fair in November 1959. When I must have spent an hour in his company talking about the old days. In my report at the time, I commented on the physical and mental fitness of this grand old showman.

Richard here, receiving a gift.

Ah! Richard Townsend,
Will you go to Sutton Club
At the end of Whitsun week?
Will the kids all be riding on your Noah's Ark and
Will the lights be shining brightly long after dark,
When we have parted with our pennies,
You will pack up and then pull out
And take your swings and fairings.
To other scenes no doubt.
Till the golden tints of autumn
Give place to winter sere,
Then come again next summer as you've done for many a year.

A gentleman from Somerset wrote this for him.

Death of 'The Guv'nor' at Weymouth

WELL-KNOWN throughout the West Country, Mr. Richard Townsend, whose death was announced in the " Echo " yesterday, remained up to his death at the age of 94, head of the firm of Richard Townsend and Sons, amusement caterers.

Mr. Townsend, who died ten days after the death of his 13-year-old granddaughter Joan, made his headquarters at Weymouth more than 60 years ago.

G.O.M. OF SHOWMEN'S GUILD

Believed to be the oldest active member of the Showmen's Guild of Great Britain and Ireland, he was known to everyone as "The Guv'nor." He was a beach tenant of Weymouth Corporation in the days of Queen Victoria, and the firm still has children's amusements on the beach.

Mr. Townsend was born in the business—it was founded by his father—and devoted his whole life to it. When he first came to Weymouth he operated a fairground on sites near where the Sidney Hall now stands. Later he ran a permanent fairground for many years in Commercial-road.

HIT BY WARS BUT SURVIVED

The firm was badly hit by the two world wars, but survived through these difficult times to get on its feet again in the post-war years.

Although in his nineties, Mr. Townsend travelled to fairgrounds in many parts of the West up to a short time before his death. And although he was taken ill at Chard Farm in May, he continued to travel to other fairs between then and the time he died. The headquarters at Weymouth is at The Depot, Putton-lane, Charlestown.

The funeral tomorrow will be at Weymouth-avenue Cemetery, Dorchester, where his wife, Mrs. Kate Townsend, was buried ten years ago.

Mr. Townsend is survived by four sons, two daughters and six grandchildren.

DEATH OF MR. RICHARD TOWNSEND

Believed to be one of the oldest active members of the Showmen's Guild, if not the oldest, Mr. Richard Townsend, head of the firm of Messrs. Richard Townsend and Sons, amusement caterers, died at Weymouth on Wednesday, August 10, at the age of 94.

He was known to fair-ground travellers and fans as "The Guv'nor."

You will notice in the report above, that the family experienced two bereavements close together, Sadly, we also lost Joan Townsend who was only 13 at the time and was one of the 4th generation like myself.

CHAPTER 16

1989 Sold, But We Still Have Our Memories

I have tried to draw a picture of a way of life that seams to fascinate many people. In years to come our future generations will start to wonder about their roots and it will all be here for them to read.

So how would I describe our way of life? Do not think for one minute it was a glamorous life, because it was not.

In the early years, in the beginning, William Townsend only got his little ride because he needed the money to survive when he lost his job on the mail stage. His son, Richard due to his lack of education, continued in the business like his father, as it was only what he knew.

Then as Richard and Kate's children (the 3rd generation) were born, travelling around had become a way of life, and Richard's children had to work hard. As during my father's time, steam travel was slow, and hard,

They were not happy days, so much so that my dad, Joe, did not wish to talk much about his young life.

Now things have changed, a showman's life is not as hard as it was then.

And yes, we the 4th generation have continued to follow on in this life, as again it was the only life we knew, or wanted to know for that matter.

It has been our family's way of life for so long, that travelling is part of us. From the very beginning in William's day, there have been Times of hardship in our business. Still we carry on.

Our upbringing has been so different to other children. Even as children, from a early age we all had to do something within the business. As soon as we could count, we were taught how to serve and count the change and I could help bag up the money for the bank before I could read. As for education, due to our father's occupation, we only went to school when we were able, which was from November to April.

Over the years Richard and Kate's children gradually passed away, and only their second born, Tom remained.

So he became the sole owner of Richard Townsend & Sons and the 4th generation took care that all carried on as usual.

In 1989, due to my Uncle Tom's age and health, a large amount of the business was sold to a dealer, which marked the end of an era for us. Life moves on sometimes without you realising it.

When the older generation dies, they take their memories and stories with them, and they are lost forever.

However, with help of members of my family and myself who can remember being told the stories and what it was like years ago, I have made it that through this book, that my family's memories will continue to live.

Now that all the rides and things we were brought up with have gone, I wish I had taken more notice of what we had, and savoured every moment of it.

What I would not give to go back in time for just one day with all the family together again. My advice to any showmen now is, treasure every moment of today, as all could be gone tomorrow.

What I do know is, the Travelling Showmen are slowly declining, and I have had the privilege to have such a life, which I would not change for anything on this earth. I was once told what we did yesterday, makes us who we are tomorrow, and that is very true when it comes to my family.

Any feedback on this book
would be most welcome

If you have memories, or stories, perhaps passed down the family, of any of your transport, be it lorry or traction engine, or even fairs, similar to this book, I would be very pleased to hear from you.

Or if you have any photos, please send them to: kay58@fsmail.net

Contact me via telephone on: 01305 778693

My Family

My daughters, Victoria (left) and Joe (right).

Ancestors

If you could see your ancestors all standing in a row,
Would you be proud of them,
Or don't you really know?

Some strange discoveries are made when climbing family trees,
Some of them do not particularly please,
If you could see your ancestors all standing in a row,
There may be some you would not like to know.

But there is another question,
That requires another view,
If your ancestors were looking back,
Would they be proud of you?

(Author unknown)

My Cousins

Jill

Paddy

Marshall

Jimmy

ACKNOWLEDGEMENTS

I would like to thank my family for their help in compiling this book, including Mr Denny Cave and my husband for his patience throughout.

Without their help, it would not have been possible.

Also, I would like to thank:

Mr Douglas Dench, for his research of the history and dates in Chapter 1

Mr Stephen Smith and the Fairground Heritage, for information and pictures in Chapters 1 & 2

Mr Peter Legg, for engine details

Mr & Mrs Brian Burden, for their help in Chapter 4 (Steam and Our Queen)

Mr Brian Andrews, for Chapter 13 (Dodgems).

Also my thanks to:

Mrs Maureen Attwooll for help with the manuscript

For pictures taken by the late Alen Imber

Ann Townsend for her wagon sketches.

I must thank the friends that have helped with information in this book and photos supplied by many people. Their help has been invaluable.

Every care has been taken, that the material within this book, does not infringe copyrights. I would like to apologise if any information or material in this publication may offend anyone. Unaccredited photos are from the Kay Townsend collection.